AIR FRYER
COOKBOOK

NEW EDITION
Over
— 220 —
*photos and
recipes, including
gluten free!*

In the
KITCHEN
ALLISON WAGGONER

NATIONAL TELEVISION HOST, CHEF, AND AUTHOR OF THE
IN THE KITCHEN SERIES: *A COLLECTION OF HOME & FAMILY MEMORIES,
A GATHERING OF FRIENDS,* AND *MULTICOOKER COOKBOOK*

FRONT TABLE BOOKS | AN IMPRINT OF CEDAR FORT, INC. | SPRINGVILLE, UTAH

ISBN 13: 978-1-4621-1961-5

Published by Front Table Books, an imprint of Cedar Fort, Inc.
2373 W. 700 S., Springville, UT 84663
Distributed by Cedar Fort, Inc., www.cedarfort.com

The Library of Congress has cataloged the earlier edition as follows:

Waggoner, Allison, 1966- author.
In the kitchen. Air fryer cooking / Allison Waggoner.
pages cm
Includes index.
ISBN 978-1-4621-1809-0 (hardback)
1. Roasting. 2. Hot air frying. I. Title. II. Title: Air fryer cooking.
TX690.W34 2015
641.7'1--dc23
                    2015026285

Cover and page design by M. Shaun McMurdie
Cover design © 2016 Cedar Fort, Inc.
Edited by Justin Greer

Printed in the United States of America

10 9 8 7 6 5 4 3 2 1

Printed on acid-free paper

www.cedarfort.com

For Bonnie Waggoner

But for you, none of this was possible. We love and miss you every moment.

Contents

Introduction

Welcome to the magnificent world of air frying.

Air fryers are revolutionary kitchen appliances that use superheated air to fry foods. But that is just the tip of the food you can cook in your air fryer.

We love the taste of deep-fried foods but not the calories or mess. Air frying is an exceptional way to cook foods fast, easy, and in less time. It heats up quickly and circulates hot air internally to cook foods and uniformly seal in all the natural juices. Air fryers allow you to fry, bake, grill, or steam food healthier, faster, and more conveniently.

This recipe book features breakfasts, vegetables, sides, main dishes, and even desserts! These are just some of the food you will be able to cook in your air fryer. This book will work with every size and style of air fryer. You can also prepare them with induction air cooking. Let these recipes inspire you to cook healthy, well-balanced meals for you and your family.

Frequently Asked Questions

Air Frying

We love the taste of deep-fried foods but not the calories or mess. Air frying is an exceptional way to cook foods fast, easy, and in less time. It heats up quickly and circulates hot air internally to cook food and uniformly seal in all the natural juices. Air fryers allow you to fry, bake, grill, and steam healthier, faster, and more conveniently.

Cooking Times

Actual cooking times in your air fryer will vary depending on several factors: the make and size of your machine, the size of food you are cooking, the thickness of cuts, the cookware used, and the temperature of items going into the air fryer basket.

As you are learning how your machine works, test the food for "doneness" before removing it from the oven. You can use a thermometer if possible. You can always start with less time and gradually adjust. When adapting a conventional recipe, slightly adjust your time cooking in an air fryer by cooking it for 20–30 percent less time.*

Bakeware

Always check with your specific machine's instructions before using any bakeware with your machine. But in most models, you can use metal, glass, and silicone. If you are looking for the ultimate crunchy and fried feel, you will want to cook your items in the air fry basket for the hot air to circulate all around your food.

Oil Sprays or Misters for Frying

Never pour oil into your machine for frying. This appliance is not to be used as a deep fryer. We recommend using good quality oil sprays or your own choice of oil in a mister when you need to spritz your food. You can use any oil: olive, canola, vegetable, or coconut. You can also use the spray in the bottom of the mesh cooking basket before cooking for easy cleanup.

Breading Foods

For foods that require breading, coat these items in small batches. Press the breading onto the food to ensure that it adheres. Spritz these items with your oil spray or mister. If breading becomes too dry, pieces may become airborne, causing smoke in the heating element.

Steaming

Check with your air fryer's instruction manual first before steaming. Most air fryers will steam food. Pour ½ cup water or broth into the bottom of your cooking basket.

*Consuming raw or undercooked meats, poultry, seafood, shellfish, or eggs may increase your risk of foodborne illness.

Air Fryer Cooking Guide

		Time (Minimum to Maximum)	Temperature (Fahrenheit)	Turn or Shake Halfway through Cooking?
Thin Frozen Fries		12–16	390	y
Thick Frozen Fries		12–20	390	y
Homemade Fries		15–25	400	y
Potato Wedges		15–25	400	y
Potato Chips		10–12	400	y
Roasted Vegetables		16–25	350	y
Cheese Sticks		8–10	400	y
Chicken Nuggets		6–10	390	y
Fish Sticks		6–10	390	y
Steak		8–12	360	y
Pork Chops		10–14	370	y
Hamburger		7–15	360	y
Chicken Wings		18–22	360	y
Drumsticks		18–22	370	y
Chicken Breast		10–15	360	y
Spareribs		18–25	410	y
Shellfish		12–15	360–400	y

Bakeware for Your Air Fryer

When purchasing an air fryer, you won't need much to get started. Most foods can be set directly in the air fryer basket. Your air fryer can bake, steam, brown, and roast to perfection, and you just need a few additional pieces of bakeware to expand your cooking options.

All types of bakeware should work in your air fryer. Carefully read your instruction booklet for any tips for your individual air fryer. As you begin planning recipes and choosing the best suitable bakeware, always consider safety, durability, cost, and functionality.

Air fryer technology utilizes hot air, circulating around food to lock in flavors while keeping food light and crispy for that classic fried taste. When you want to accomplish a "fried" finish, set aside the bakeware and place the food directly into the air fryer basket.

When using glass or metal bakeware, your air fryer will function more like a traditional oven. But remember, air fryers work at different times and temperatures, and you'll need to adjust recipes when adapting traditional oven-baked dishes into new air fried recipes. Most commonly, large and deep pans will be closer to the heating element that normally sits in the top of the unit. Try out different temperatures and settings to make sure food is not too close to the heating element when cooking.

The most important thing to remember is that each air fryer is unique and might have slight variations in heat settings or calibrations. Even similarly branded air fryers may differ in cooking capacity. An easy rule of cooking in an air fryer: If something is browning too fast or the insides of your dishes are not cooked throughout, turn the temperature down and extend your cooking time. If you are cooking large items, like a roast or turkey breast, keep the heat lower and turn your food often. As you begin testing and adjusting recipes with your own air fryer, keep notes in your cookbooks based on time or temperature adjustments to keep your recipes consistently delicious.

Bakeware Guide

	Heat Time	Cooling	Nonstick	Foods	Dishwasher Recommended	Cook Time Variations	Notes
Nonstick	Fast	Fast	Yes	All	Yes	If you're concerned about too much or too fast browning, lower your temperature	The darker the color, the faster your items will brown
Aluminum	Fast	Fast	No	Do not use with acidic foods like citrus and tomato	No	Make sure to use a nonstick spray and/or parchment to line pans	Great conductor of heat
Glass	Fast	Fast	No	All	Yes	Lower your cooking temperature and time	Use caution when going from hot to cold, as glass can shatter or break
Silicone	Very Fast	Very Fast	Yes	All	Yes		Handle with care when transferring items to the oven, as silicone is a bit flimsy by nature
Enameled Cast Iron	Slow	Slow	Yes	All	No	Add time to your items, as these vessels take longer to heat	Don't choose this if you are looking to brown on the bottom
Parchment Paper	Fast	Fast	Semi	All	No (recycle)		Easy choice to line pans or the bottom of your air fryer basket with something that is very messy or sticky or would fall through the basket

How to Choose the Right Oils

There are many oils on the market today. Trying new oils can be as thrilling as experimenting with a new seasoning on your favorite dish. Oils can ignite unreleased flavor or make a dish sing with fragrance.

When choosing oil, you need to first determine whether you're using the oil to cook your dish or just flavor it. Making this determination will allow you to prepare and utilize oil at the right temperature while obtaining the best flavor.

Every cooking oil has a threshold smoke point when the oil begins to break down—otherwise known as each oil's magical number. When using an air fryer, look for oils with higher smoke points to properly prepare your dish without sacrificing the delicious flavor components of the oil. Most smoke points are determined based on the elements of filtered and refined oils. Unfiltered and unrefined oils will have lower smoke points. As you increase the temperature in your cooking, you should use an oil with a higher smoke point.

Delicate oils , like walnut, dark sesame, pistachio, hazelnut, pumpkin seed, and pecan, usually have a low smoke point. If the oil is heated, its distinct flavors can be destroyed. You will find that delicate oils are best served chilled or used to finish a hot dish for flavor.

Notably, some oils are made in both dark and light compositions to allow for varied uses. For example, sesame oils can come in dark and light. The lighter sesame oil has a higher smoke point and can be used in an air fryer, while the darker sesame oil has a lower smoke point and should be used to provide finishing flavors to a dish.

When storing oils, always try for a dark, cool cabinet away from heat. Most oils will only last twelve months before expiring. Your nose will tell you if an oil is past its prime, or you can simply note the purchase date with a marker on each container. This will allow you to utilize a variety of oils before you lose them to time.

Oils allow you to be creative in your cooking. Try a new twist on a classic dish with a new oil or seasoning. You'll be surprised how a drop or two of your favorite fragrant oil can enhance or change your dish completely!

Oil Guide

Oil	Smoke Point	Air Fry	Finish	Saute	Vinaigrette	Notes
Avocado Oil	510°F (265°C)	●	●	●	●	Very high smoke point with great flavor
Canola Oil	400°F (205°C)	●		●	●	Neutral, all purpose
Coconut Oil	350°F (175°C)	●		●		Soild at room temperature, great subsitute to create vegan dishes, but not great for vinaigrettes or finishing
Corn Oil	450°F (230°C)	●		●		Neutral, all purpose
Extra Virgin Olive Oil	325°F (165°C)		●		●	Depending on the origin, you can have beautiful nutty, spicy, fruity flavors; use to finish the dish
Grapeseed Oil	390°F (195°C)	●		●	●	Neutral, all purpose
Hemp Seed Oil	n/a		●		●	Very sensitive to heating, use to finish only
Light Olive Oil	465°F (240°C)	●		●	●	
Palm Oil	450°F (230°C)			●		
Peanut Oil	450°F (230°C)	●		●		Different from most other nut oils because it has a much higher smoke point
Pistachio Oil	n/a		●		●	Very sensitive to heating, use to finish only
Pumpkin Seed Oil	n/a		●		●	Very sensitive to heating, use to finish only
Sesame oil	410°F (210°C)	●	●	●	●	
Sesame Oil – Toasted (Dark)	n/a		●		●	Very sensitive to heating, use to finish only
Sunflower Oil	440°F (450°F)	●		●	●	
Truffle Oil	n/a		●			Very sensitive to heating, use to finish only
Vegetable Oil	450°F (230°C)	●		●	●	Neutral, all purpose
Walnut Oil	325°F (165°C)		●			Very sensitive to heating, use to finish only
Safflower Oil	510°F (265°C)	●		●	●	Almost flavorless, all purpose
Rice Bran Oil	490°F (260°C)	●		●	●	Neutral, all purpose, good non-GMO oil

Gluten Free in Your Air Fryer

Many dishes in this book are gluten free or can be made gluten free. For those of you with specific allergies, make sure to always check with your doctor for instructions on what you can and cannot eat.

Many items that we like to cook are breaded in an air fryer. We found that gluten-free cereals, like Rice Chex, and pork rinds are among the fastest and crunchiest coatings you can substitute. You can pulse these in your food processor into a crisp coating in place of panko.

Also, here's a great flour combination that we like to use as a substitute for flour in breading some of your favorites.

All-Purpose Gluten-Free Flour Mix

makes 12 cups

8 cups rice flour
2⅔ cups potato starch flour
1⅓ cups tapioca flour

On the following page, you'll find a list of some gluten-free flours that you may choose to use in your cooking!

Throughout this book you'll see two different gluten-free symbols.

This one means that the recipe is already gluten-free.

This one means that it can easily be made gluten-free with a simple substitution, which you'll find explained in the tip below the recipe. Of course, always check the recipes yourself, as it's often difficult to determine whether some products and ingredients are really gluten-free.

Gluten-Free Flours

Flour	Notes
Amaranth Flour	This protein-rich flour is derived from grinding the seeds of the amaranth plant. Nutty flavor.
Arrowroot	A white flour from the root of the West Indian plant of the same name. Mostly used in place of cornstarch.
Bean Flours	Including garbanzo bean flour and Romano bean flour, these flours are typically high in protein and have a distinct flavor. They are better suited for heartier recipes, such as bread.
Buckwheat Flour	It has a distinct taste, which makes it best when combined with other, more bland flours. A little goes a long way. Mostly used in pancakes or baking.
Coconut Flour	Ground from dried coconut meat into a fine powder. It lends a pleasant flavor to baked goods.
Corn Flour	Made from ground corn, this flour is too coarse for baking, but is very nice for pancakes, cornbread, and tortillas, or for breading.
Millet Flour	This nutrient-rich flour is ground from the grain of the same name. It has a subtle flavor and can be used for sweet or savory baking.
Nut Flours	Choose a nut, choose any nut. Now, grind it into a fine powder. That's what nut flours are. They cannot be substituted in equal quantities for flour because they are dense. But they're fun to work with for great flavor.
Potato Starch Flour	Made from ground potatoes, this is a fine, white powder. It is popular for cakes and more delicate baked goods.
Quinoa Flour	The coating on the seeds of this grain, from which the flour is milled, is traditionally very bitter. Look to see if you can find a debittered version. Great for baked goods and is well suited for scones and biscuits and pancakes.
Rice Flours	Rice flours are a key ingredient in most gluten-free baking.
Sorghum Flour	Made from sorghum, which is a relative of sugarcane. It's tender and adds a mild sweetness but is rarely used alone.
Soy Flour	Made from ground soybeans, this flour has a nutty flavor and high protein content. It can be used to replace a portion of flour in recipes or can be used as a thickener. However, this type of flour can tend to make baked goods brown more rapidly, so keep an eye on bake times.
Tapioca Flour	From the root of the cassava plant, this is light, starchy flour, which adds a superior texture and "chew" to baked goods. It is frequently used in gluten-free baking, along with other flours.
Xanthan Gum	This is not flour, but since it's something that you'll see very frequently in gluten-free recipes, it bears mentioning. This is a powder milled from *xanthomonas campestris*. It replaces the gluten in breads and baking with gluten-free flours.

Breakfast

Blueberry Dutch Babies

⅔ cup fresh blueberries

1 cup milk

¾ cup flour

¼ cup sugar

2 eggs

1 tsp. vanilla extract

¼ tsp. baking powder

⅛ tsp. salt

Divide the blueberries into 12 buttered silicone muffin cups.

Place all other ingredients in a bowl and whisk until smooth. Divide among the 12 cups, filling only halfway. Place cups in a single layer in the air fryer basket. Do not crowd. Back at 350 degrees for 12-15 minutes until lightly browned. Dust with powdered sugar.

Strawberry and Cream Cheese French Toast Roll-Ups, page 5

Strawberry and Cream Cheese French Toast Roll-Ups

8 slices white sandwich bread

8 Tbsp. cream cheese, softened

8 strawberries, sliced thin

2 eggs

3 Tbsp. milk

⅓ cup sugar

1 tsp. ground cinnamon

Cut the crust from each slice of bread and flatten it out with a rolling pin.

Place about 1 tablespoon of cream cheese in a strip starting 1 inch from one end of the bread. Top with the sliced strawberries.

Roll the bread up tightly and repeat with the remaining pieces of bread.

In a shallow bowl, whisk the eggs and milk until well combined.

In a separate shallow bowl, mix the sugar with the cinnamon.

Dip each bread roll in the egg mixture, coating well, and then roll each one in the sugar mixture.

Place in an air fryer basket seam-side down. Spray lightly with canola oil spray. Cook in batches until golden brown at 330 degrees for 5 minutes.

Biscuit Beignets with Praline Sauce

Praline Sauce

8 Tbsp. butter

1 cup brown sugar

3 Tbsp. milk

3 Tbsp. vanilla extract

¼ cup chopped nuts, pecans or
  walnuts

Beignets

1 tube large flaky-style biscuit
  dough

3 Tbsp. powdered sugar

For the Praline Sauce

Melt butter in a medium, heavy-bottomed saucepan over medium heat. Add brown sugar and whisk until sugar melts and mixture begins to boil, about 5 minutes. Stir in milk, vanilla, and nuts until smooth. Set aside.

For the Beignets

Separate biscuits and cut into fourths. Spray each side with a light spray of canola oil.

Bake at 330 degrees for 10 minutes in single layer batches so that the biscuits do not touch and have room to expand. Biscuits will cook very quickly.

Dust generously with powdered sugar and serve immediately with Praline Sauce.

Biscuit Beignets with Praline Sauce, page 6

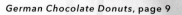
German Chocolate Donuts, page 9

German Chocolate Donuts

½ cup chocolate frosting

1 Tbsp. water

1 can large flaky-style biscuit
dough

¼ cup pecans

¼ cup flaked coconut, toasted

1 cup German chocolate frosting-
flavored frosting

In medium bowl, stir chocolate frosting and 1 tablespoon water until smooth. Set aside.

Separate dough into 8 biscuits; gently roll them down to ½ inch thick with a rolling pin. With a 1-inch round cutter, cut a hole in the center of each biscuit.

Meanwhile, in small bowl, mix pecans and coconut.

Spritz each side of each biscuit with canola oil spray.

In batches, place the biscuits in the basket in a single layer, not touching.

Bake at 330 degrees for 10 minutes until golden.

Lift donuts out of the basket with tongs and frost each top with German chocolate frosting. With a spoon, drizzle the previously prepared chocolate frosting over the top.

Sprinkle with pecan mixture. Serve warm or cool.

Note: This is a great basic for all things donuts—you can top them with just chocolate or add coconut or nuts. This list is endless!

Lemon Blueberry Coffee Cake

Cake

½ cup quick or old-fashioned
rolled oats

1 cup flour

¼ cup brown sugar

1 Tbsp. baking powder

1 Tbsp. finely grated lemon peel

2 Tbsp. all-vegetable shortening

½ cup milk

2 large egg whites, lightly beaten

½ cup blueberries, fresh or frozen,
well drained

Glaze

¼ cup powdered sugar

1–2 tsp. lemon juice

1 tsp. finely grated lemon peel

For the Cake

Lightly spray 2 mini loaf pans or 2 individual pot pie pans with a canola spray.

Place oats in a blender or food processor and process about 1 minute. It will look like a coarse flour.

Combine oats, flour, brown sugar, baking powder, and lemon peel in large bowl. Add shortening with a fork, mixing in until mixture resembles coarse crumbs.

Stir in milk and egg whites just until blended. Fold in blueberries. Spoon into prepared pans.

Bake 1 pan at a time at 300 degrees for 15 minutes. Cool slightly. (Since this makes 2, you may need to cook them in batches. Freeze one for later!)

For the Glaze

Mix powdered sugar and lemon juice in small bowl. Drizzle over coffee cake. Sprinkle with lemon peel.

Lemon Blueberry Coffee Cake, page 10

Bacon and Egg Crescent Squares

1 can refrigerated crescent roll

4 eggs

2 slices bacon, cut in half widthwise, then halved lengthwise

4 tsp. grated Parmesan cheese, divided

salt and pepper

1 Tbsp. fresh chopped basil

Open and unroll the crescents onto a clean dry surface. Split the dough right down the middle, then in half to form 4 rectangles. Pinch the perforations together in each rectangle.

Fold up the edges of each section of dough (about ½-inch edge around each rectangle). Place 1 rectangle in the air fryer basket and crack 1 egg into the center of it. Place 2 of the bacon sections across the egg on each square. Sprinkle with 1 teaspoon of Parmesan cheese and salt and pepper to taste. Add a portion of the basil.

Bake in the oven at 300 degrees for 10 minutes, until the edges of the crescent dough are golden brown and the egg is cooked to your preference. Repeat with remaining dough sections (baking in batches as needed, not letting the squares touch in the air fryer).

Crispy Cheesy Hash Brown Casserole

½ (10.5-oz.) can cream of chicken soup

½ cup sour cream

½ tsp. salt

1½ cups shredded hash brown potatoes

⅓ cup chopped onion

1 cup shredded cheddar cheese

½ cup breadcrumbs

2 Tbsp. butter, melted

2 scallions, finely chopped (optional)

In a large bowl, whisk together soup, sour cream, and salt. Stir in hash browns, onions, and cheese until well mixed. Spoon evenly into a 6-inch square baking dish.

In a medium bowl, mix together breadcrumbs and butter. Sprinkle evenly on top of hash brown mixture.

Bake uncovered for about 15 minutes at 300 degrees, or until hot and bubbly. Allow to rest for 5 minutes before serving. Garnish with sliced scallions if desired.

Greek Feta Baked Omelet

3 eggs, lightly beaten

3 Tbsp. frozen leaf spinach, thawed and drained

2 Tbsp. crumbled feta cheese

6 cherry tomatoes, quartered

⅛ tsp. oregano

Spray a 6-inch square baking dish with nonstick spray. Pour in eggs and top with spinach, cheese, and tomatoes. Sprinkle the top with oregano.

Bake at 330 degrees for 8–10 minutes.

Maple-Glazed Donuts

1 can large flaky-style biscuit dough

¼ cup butter, melted

1½ cups powdered sugar

2 tsp. maple extract

1–2 Tbsp. milk

Separate dough into 8 biscuits. With a 1-inch round cutter, cut a hole in the center of each biscuit. Dip both sides of each biscuit in melted butter; place on a cookie sheet. (You can also dip the holes in the butter and place on the cookie sheet.)

Bake in an air fryer basket in batches at 330 degrees for 10–12 minutes or until golden brown. Remove donuts (and holes) from the basket to the cooling rack. Cool about 15 minutes.

In medium bowl, place powdered sugar and maple extract. Add 1 tablespoon milk; stir until combined. If needed for dipping consistency, stir in remaining milk. Dip each donut (and hole) halfway into icing. Place on cooling rack placed over paper-lined cookie sheet.

Baked Eggs in Brioche

3 brioche rolls (about 3×3 inches in size)

3 Tbsp. butter, melted

3 slices American cheese, or cheddar

salt and pepper, to taste

3 eggs

1 Tbsp. chives

Cut off tops of brioche (about 1 inch) and scoop out insides of bottoms to make a shell, leaving ¼ to ½ inch all around and being careful not to tear. The inside opening should be just big enough for 1 large egg. Brush insides and cut edges of tops with butter. Add 1 slice of cheese to the inside of each roll.

Arrange brioche shells in air fryer basket and season with salt and pepper. Crack an egg into each brioche and sprinkle with chives. Bake brioche 7-9 minutes at 330 degrees.

Serve each brioche with its top for dipping in egg.

Tip: These can be made gluten-free by substituting a gluten-free roll for the brioche rolls.

Baked Eggs in Brioche, page 14

Morning Cheese Danish, page 17

Morning Cheese Danish

1 (8-oz.) pkg. cream cheese, room temperature

⅓ cup sugar

3 eggs, room temperature, divided

2 Tbsp. ricotta cheese

1 tsp. vanilla extract

¼ tsp. salt

1 Tbsp. grated lemon zest

2 sheets prepared puff pastry, defrosted

1 Tbsp. water

cherry preserves

In an electric mixer, combine the cream cheese and sugar on a low speed. With the mixer still on a low speed, add two egg yolks, ricotta cheese, vanilla extract, salt, and lemon zest. Mix until combined. Do not over mix or whip.

On a lightly floured cutting board, unroll 1 sheet of the puff pastry. Line a cookie sheet with parchment paper. Cut the puff pastry into square pieces, approximately 6 inches, and place, separated, on the cookie sheet. Then place a tablespoon of the cheese mixture into the middle of each square.

In a small bowl, combine 1 beaten egg and 1 tablespoon water to make an egg wash. Brush the borders of each pastry with the egg wash. Fold 2 opposite corners toward the center of each pastry so they touch and stick together. Brush the top of each pastry with the egg wash. Repeat this with the second sheet of puff pastry.

Refrigerate for 20 minutes.

Bake at 330 degrees for 10–15 minutes until the pastries are lightly brown. Bake in batches as needed. When cooled, add a spoonful of cherry preserves on the top and serve!

Egg & Cheese Strata

3 slices whole wheat bread

1 large egg, lightly beaten

½ cup whole milk

½ cup grated cheddar cheese, divided

sea salt

black pepper

1 thin slices prosciutto

3 asparagus spears, cut into 5-inch lengths (tops only)

1 Tbsp. chopped chives

Butter a small 4-cup ovenproof baking dish.

Remove the crusts from the bread and cut into cubes; you should have about 1½ cups. Place the cubes into the baking dish.

Whisk together the eggs and milk in a large bowl. Stir in half of the cheese and season with salt and pepper. Pour ¾ of the egg mixture over the bread cubes.

Cut the prosciutto into 1-inch squares and lay over the coated bread and top with asparagus spears. Pour the remaining egg mixture over the top and top with the remaining cheese.

Bake the strata at 330 degrees until just set, 15 minutes. Let cool slightly, sprinkle with the chopped chives, and serve in the baking dish.

Tip: This can be made gluten-free by substituting gluten-free bread for the whole wheat bread.

Egg & Cheese Strata, page 18

Parmesan Baked Eggs, page 21

Parmesan Baked Eggs

3 Tbsp. butter
1 Tbsp. minced fresh rosemary
½ Tbsp. minced fresh thyme
1 shallot, minced
6 tsp. heavy cream

6 eggs
3 Tbsp. grated Parmesan cheese
salt and pepper, to taste

In 3 small ramekins, evenly divide and place the butter, rosemary, thyme, and shallot. Place the ramekins in an air fryer basket and heat at 350 degrees for 2 minutes until melted.

Remove the air basket from the fryer. Add 2 teaspoons heavy cream to each ramekin and crack 2 eggs into each ramekin without breaking the yolks. Sprinkle the cheese over the top of each ramekin and return to the oven. Bake for 7-9 minutes at 350 degrees.

Remove from oven when the egg whites are just set and yolks are still soft. Let stand for 3-5 minutes before serving. Season with salt and pepper.

Sweet-and-Spicy Bacon, page 25

Sweet-and-Spicy Bacon

1 lb. thick-cut bacon (about 12
  slices)

1½ Tbsp. brown sugar

¼ tsp. cayenne pepper

¼ tsp. black pepper

Cut the bacon in 2 or 3 equal sections to fit along the air fryer basket.

Stir together the brown sugar, cayenne, and black pepper in a bowl. Add the
bacon a few slices at a time until all slices are covered in the mixture.

Arrange the bacon slices in 1 layer (not overlapping) in the basket.

Bake at 350 degrees for 6–8 minutes in batches.

Salted Caramel Flake Donut

1 can crescent dinner rolls

1 (4-oz.) can vanilla pudding

2 Tbsp. caramel ice cream
  topping

¼ tsp. kosher salt

½ cup powdered sugar

1–2 Tbsp. milk

Separate crescent dough into 4 rectangles. Firmly press perforations together
to seal. Stack 2 rectangles on top of one another. Fold in half widthwise to
make a tall stack. Repeat with remaining 2 rectangles.

To make 2 donuts, use a 3-inch biscuit cutter to cut 1 round from each stack;
use a ½-inch biscuit cutter to a cut small hole in the center of each round.
Reroll and reform remaining dough to cut third donut.

Place in air fryer basket in a single layer and spray each side lightly with canola
oil. Bake at 330 degrees for 10 minutes. Cool for 5 minutes.

Carefully split donuts in half. Place pudding in a plastic bag with the corner
cut off and pipe some pudding onto the bottom half of each donut. Top each
with some caramel sauce and sprinkle with salt. Cover with each donut top.

In a small bowl, mix powdered sugar and enough milk for spreading
consistency. Spread on donut tops. Drizzle with additional caramel sauce.

*Note: Substitute the caramel ice cream topping with the Homemade Salted Caramel
Sauce on page 27 for an extra treat!*

Homemade Salted Caramel Sauce, page 27

Homemade Salted Caramel Sauce
(Use with Salted Caramel Flake Donut, page 25)

1 cup sugar

¼ cup water

1 tsp. light-colored corn syrup

½ cup heavy whipping cream

1 Tbsp. vanilla extract

½ tsp. salt

Gather all your ingredients and tools in one place, including oven mitts and a glass jar or heat-safe container. You'll be working with boiling sugar and will need to watch over it carefully.

In a medium to large stainless steel saucepan (it should be much bigger than you think you'll need because the sauce will bubble very vigorously toward the end of the cooking), add the sugar, water, and corn syrup. Bring it to a boil over high heat, whisking until sugar has dissolved.

Allow the mixture to boil for 5–12 minutes so it can turn caramel-colored. The final stage is where the mixture turns from pale amber to that perfect shade of caramel. This stage can go quickly, in less than 30 seconds, so don't take your eyes off it! While boiling, you don't want to whisk, but you can gently stir. As soon as the sauce has turned caramel-colored, reduce the heat to low.

Very carefully and slowly, add the cream. You need to do this with caution because the mixture will bubble up. Repeat this step with the vanilla and salt.

Whisk until sauce is smooth and combined. Let it boil another minute, which helps thicken it up.

Transfer the sauce to a glass jar or heat-safe container. Allow the sauce to cool uncovered to room temperature; the sauce thickens considerably as it cools. The sauce will keep airtight at room temperature for at least 1 month.

Sausage, Egg, and Cheese Breakfast Roll-Ups

3 eggs

1 can refrigerated crescent rolls

8 breakfast sausage links, cooked

4 slices cheddar cheese

salt and pepper, to taste

In a small bowl, beat the eggs. Reserve 2 tablespoons beaten egg for brushing on the tops of the crescent rolls.

Scramble remaining eggs.

Unroll the dough onto a work surface. Separate the dough into 8 triangles. Cut the cheese slices in half. Place 1 half on each triangle. Top each with 1 spoonful of scrambled eggs and 1 sausage link. Loosely roll up the triangles as directed on the can.

Place roll-ups, in batches, in an ungreased air fryer basket.

Brush the reserved beaten egg on top of each crescent. Sprinkle salt and pepper over each.

Bake at 330 degrees for 12–15 minutes.

Note: You can double this recipe up and freeze any remaining roll-ups. They heat up beautifully from frozen in your air fryer in 4–5 minutes on those busy mornings!

Air-Dried Herbs

Take any herbs you would like. Wash and set them in an air fryer basket.

You may want to put your rack on top of the herbs as they dry. Be patient, because this will give you great results as you fine-tune the time on your machine.

Bake at 170 degrees for 20 minutes. You will need to watch over these carefully. Depending on the size and cut of herbs, you may need to go more or less time. Set them on a baking sheet overnight to cool. Store them in an airtight container.

Avocado and Feta Egg Rolls

Egg Rolls

24 egg roll wrappers

2 ripe avocados, cut into ¼-inch pieces

4 Tbsp. chopped sun-dried tomatoes

¼ cup feta cheese

½ Tbsp. finely chopped garlic

salt and pepper, to taste

Sauce

1 avocado

¼ cup buttermilk

2 Tbsp. Greek yogurt

2 Tbsp. freshly squeezed lime juice

1 Tbsp. chopped fresh cilantro

1 tsp. minced garlic

For the Egg Rolls

In a large mixing bowl, lightly stir together the chopped avocado, sun-dried tomatoes, feta, garlic, salt, and pepper.

Working with 1 wrapper at a time, place 1 tablespoon of filling in the wrap. Brush the edges with water and roll like a burrito. Seal with more water. Repeat until all rolls are complete.

Lightly spray with canola oil on all sides.

Bake for 10–12 minutes at 400 degrees in a single layer, turning once during cooking.

For the Sauce

Place all ingredients into a food processor and process until smooth.

Bloomin' Onion Straws

1 large sweet onion, sliced very
   thin

large bowl of ice water

1 cup self-rising flour

1 tsp. salt

1 tsp. pepper

1 tsp. paprika

1 tsp. garlic powder

canola oil spray

Let the onions soak in the ice water for at least 10 minutes.

In a gallon-size ziplock bag, mix the flour with the salt, pepper, paprika, and garlic powder.

Using a pair of tongs, remove the onions from the ice water. Shake off excess water. Place the onions in the bag and toss in the seasoned flour.

Remove the onions from the bag and shake off all the excess flour. Place an even row of onions in the basket. Do not overcrowd. Evenly spray the onions with canola oil spray.

Bake in batches at 410 degrees for 14 minutes. After 7 minutes, turn the onions and spray again with oil.

Tip: These can be made gluten-free by substituting gluten-free flour for the regular flour.

Bloomin' Onion Sauce

1 cup mayonnaise

3 Tbsp. chili sauce

1 tsp. chili powder

⅛ tsp. cayenne pepper

Mix together and chill.

Kale Chips, page 39

Kale Chips

1 large bunch kale   canola oil spray

Wash and dry the kale. Remove the large rib in the center of each leaf. Cut each leaf into 1-inch pieces.

Spray them lightly with canola or olive oil spray. Season the kale with either salt and pepper or your favorite seasoning.

Bake at 250 degrees for 15 minutes, tossing halfway through.

Note: You can use any type of oil you want! You can even use sesame oil for a fun nutty taste.

Baked Brie with Figs, Walnuts, and Pistachios

4 Tbsp. fig preserves or jam,
  divided

⅓ cup sliced dried figs   ⅓ cup chopped walnuts

⅓ cup chopped pistachio nuts   13 oz. brie cheese round

Place the fig jam or preserves in a microwave-safe dish. Microwave for 30 seconds to soften.

In a small bowl, combine the sliced dried figs with the nuts. Add half of the fig jam and mix.

Place the round of brie in a 6-inch oven-safe dish. Using a knife, coat the brie with the remainder of the jam.

Top the brie with the fig and nut mixture.

Place the brie dish in the air fryer basket. Bake at 325 degree for 10 minutes.

Serve with French bread or crackers.

Artichoke and Spinach Dip

½ (8-oz.) pkg. cream cheese, softened

⅛ cup mayonnaise

⅛ cup grated Parmesan cheese

⅛ cup grated Romano cheese

1 clove garlic, minced

¼ tsp. dried basil

¼ tsp. garlic salt

salt and pepper, to taste

½ (14-oz.) can artichoke hearts, drained and chopped

½ (10-oz.) pkg. frozen spinach, thawed, drained, and squeezed dry

⅓ cup shredded mozzarella cheese

bread bowl or pita chips

Mix together the cream cheese, mayonnaise, Parmesan, Romano, garlic, basil, garlic salt, and salt and pepper.

Gently stir in the artichoke hearts and spinach. Transfer the mixture to a 6-inch square baking dish. Sprinkle the mozzarella on top.

Bake for 15 minutes at 330 degrees, until bubbly and lightly browned on top. Serve in a bread bowl or with pita chips.

Artichoke and Spinach Dip, page 40

Spicy Stuffed Cherry Peppers, page 43

Spicy Stuffed Cherry Peppers

12 fresh red cherry peppers

1 Tbsp. olive oil

8 ounces Italian sausage, without casing

¼ cup ricotta cheese

¼ parsley, chopped

3 Tbsp. grated Parmesan cheese

1 tsp. lemon zest

1 tsp. fresh basil, chopped

1 clove garlic, minced

½ tsp. salt and pepper

½ cup mozzarella cheese

Cut the tops of the peppers off and remove the seeds. Spritz with olive oil.

Place the bottoms and tops in the air fryer basket and cook at 350 degrees for 3-5 minutes until starting to blister. Remove and let cool.

Combine sausage with ricotta and Parmesan cheeses, parsley, lemon, basil, garlic, salt, and pepper. Stuff the pepper with the mixture and top with mozzarella. Bake at 300 degrees for 10-16 minutes until cooked through, depending on the size of the peppers. Cover with roasted tops.

Broccoli with Shaved Parmesan

1 lb. broccoli, cut into 1½-inch florets

2 Tbsp. olive oil

1 tsp. kosher salt

½ tsp. ground black pepper

2 tsp. grated lemon zest

1 cup fresh spinach leaves

¼ cup shaved Parmesan cheese

Toss the florets with olive oil, salt, and pepper.

Set the air fryer to 400 degrees and place the broccoli in the air fryer basket. Cook the broccoli for 13–16 minutes, tossing halfway through the cooking process to ensure even browning.

When done, toss the broccoli in a serving bowl with lemon zest, spinach, and Parmesan cheese and serve immediately.

Broccoli with Shaved Parmesan, page 44

Bacon Cheddar Muffins, page 47

Bacon Cheddar Muffins

extra-virgin olive oil

6 slices bacon

1 box corn muffin mix, plus ingredients (according to package directions) to make 1 batch muffins

1 tsp. paprika

3-4 Tbsp. chopped chives

⅓ cup cheddar cheese, shredded

Drizzle a little extra-virgin olive oil into a small skillet and place over medium-high heat. Add the bacon to the hot pan and crisp, 5-6 minutes. Remove from pan and drain on a paper towel. Chop and set aside.

Prepare the muffin mix to package directions. Stir in the paprika, chives, shredded cheese, and crisp bacon bits.

Fill the mini muffin pan with batter and bake at 330 degrees for about 15 minutes or until golden brown.

Bacon-Wrapped Cheese-Stuffed Dates

½ lb. pitted dates
½ lb. bacon slices, cut in half
2 ounces cheese, blue or goat

Make a pocket in each date by cutting a slice down 1 side. Place a large crumble of cheese into each date pocket and pinch the openings together.

Wrap each date with a piece of bacon and secure it with a toothpick.

Place the dates in an air fryer basket and bake for about 10 minutes at 330 degrees in a single layer.

Homemade Kettle Chips with Dill Dip

Chips

4 Idaho potatoes
canola oil spray
salt and pepper, to taste

Dill Dip

½ cup sour cream
½ cup mayonnaise
¼ cup finely chopped yellow onion
½ tsp. dried dill

Using a mandoline or food processor, slice the potatoes very thin.

Place the sliced potatoes in a large bowl with cold water to soak for 30 minutes.

Make the dip by stirring all the ingredients together. Refrigerate.

Divide the potatoes into 4 batches. Lay them out on a towel and dry. Spray each side with canola oil. Season with salt and pepper.

In batches, lay the slices out in an air fryer basket. Bake at 400 degrees for 5 minutes. Open and toss. Bake for another 5 minutes until crisp.

Bacon-Wrapped Cheese-Stuffed Dates, page 48

Beer-Battered Onion Rings, page 51

Beer-Battered Onion Rings

¼ cup flour

1 Tbsp. cornstarch

½ tsp. garlic powder

¼ tsp. cayenne pepper

¼ tsp. salt

½ cup brown ale

1 cup fine yellow cornmeal

1 large sweet onion, sliced into
½-inch-thick rings

canola or olive oil cooking spray

Whisk the flour, cornstarch, garlic powder, cayenne, and salt in a medium bowl. Whisk in the ale until combined.

Place the cornmeal in a shallow bowl.

Separate the onion slices into rings and dip in the batter, letting the excess drip off. Then dredge in the cornmeal.

Place in the air fryer basket and coat the onion rings with cooking spray.

Bake in batches at 400 degrees for 6–8 minutes. Turn, coat the other side with cooking spray, and bake until browned and crispy, 6–8 minutes more.

Tip: These can be made gluten-free by substituting gluten-free flour and cornmeal for their normal counterparts.

Warm Avocado and Chilled Grapefruit Salad

2 whole avocados ripened

¼ cup heart of palm, julienne cut

3 Tbsp. olive oil

2 Tbsp. white wine vinegar

2 Tbsp. mint leaves, chopped

2 grapefruits, peeled and segmented

4 cups mixed greens

3 Tbsp. chopped pistachios

Cut avocado in half and remove seed. Place skin side down in the air fryer basket. Bake at 300 degrees for 5-7 minutes until heated through. Carefully remove and cool slightly.

In a medium bowl, whisk together the olive oil, vinegar, and mint. Cut and scoop cooled-but-still-warm avocado and place in bowl. Add the grapefruit and hearts of palm and gently toss.

Divide the mixed greens onto 4 plates. Top with the avocado mixture and sprinkle with the pistachios.

Warm Avacado and Chilled Grapefruit Salad, page 52

Roasted Butternut Squash, page 55

Roasted Butternut Squash

1–2 lb. squash, peeled, seeded, and cubed

¼ cup brown sugar

2 Tbsp. butter, melted

¾ Tbsp. fresh grated ginger

1 tsp. chopped rosemary

In a bowl, place the squash, brown sugar, butter, ginger, and rosemary. Toss until coated.

Put the squash in the air fryer basket and bake at 330 degrees for 10 minutes. Toss the squash and bake for another 8–10 minutes at 400 degrees.

Bourbon Sweet Potatoes

3 sweet potatoes, peeled and boiled until fork tender

¼ cup fine aged Kentucky bourbon whiskey

1 egg, slightly beaten

¼ cup chopped pecans

¼ cup sugar

1 Tbsp. butter

⅛ tsp. grated cinnamon

⅛ tsp. grated nutmeg

Mix all of the ingredients with an electric mixer at a medium speed until smooth.

Pour all of the ingredients into a 6-inch baking dish. Bake, lightly covered with foil, at 330 degrees for 15 minutes.

Zucchini Fritter Cakes

1 small zucchini, grated
2 Tbsp. salt
4 green onions, minced
1 Tbsp. fresh chopped parsley

1 Tbsp. fresh chopped dill
1 egg, lightly beaten
¾ cup grated Parmesan cheese
¼ cup flour

Grate the zucchini into a colander in the sink; toss with salt and let sit 10 minutes.

Rinse the zucchini off under cold water. Press down in the colander to remove excess water. This next step is very important to get the most liquid off that you can. Place the zucchini on a paper towel and squeeze until almost dry.

Mix the zucchini with the minced green onions, parsley, dill, egg, Parmesan, and flour.

Take 1 tablespoon at a time and roll into a ball. Flatten just a bit. Spray each side with canola oil. Repeat with the remaining mixture.

Bake in a single layer at 330 degrees for 10 minutes until golden. Bake in batches as needed.

Zucchini Fritter Cakes, page 56

Cheesy Potatoes au Gratin, page 59

Cheesy Potatoes au Gratin

3 medium potatoes
¼ cup milk
¼ cup cream
1 tsp. black pepper

1 tsp. nutmeg
¼ cup shredded Gruyère cheese

Slice the potatoes wafer thin. In a bowl, mix the milk, cream, pepper, and nutmeg. Add the potatoes to the mixture and coat evenly.

Place the potato slices into a 6-inch pan and pour the rest of the cream mixture on top of the potatoes. Sprinkle the cheese evenly over the potatoes.

Place the pan in the cooking basket and cook at 330 degrees for 15 minutes until browned.

Cheddar Bacon Bites

2 cups finely shredded cheddar cheese
¾ cup mayonnaise
2-3 tsp. Dijon mustard

1 can large flaky-style biscuit dough
4 slices bacon, cooked and crumbled

In a large bowl, combine the cheese, mayonnaise, and mustard.

Split each biscuit circle into thirds. Press into the bottom and up the sides of the ungreased miniature muffin cups. Fill each with about 1 tablespoon of the cheese mixture.

Bake at 300 degrees for 9–11 minutes or until golden brown and the cheese is melted. Bake in batches as needed. Let stand for 3 minutes before removing from the pans.

Buffalo Cauliflower

1 cauliflower, cut into bite-size florets

olive oil

2 tsp. garlic powder

¼ tsp. salt

⅛ tsp. pepper

1 Tbsp. butter, melted

½–¾ cup buffalo wing-style hot sauce

Place cauliflower florets into a medium-size bowl. Drizzle olive oil over florets to barely coat. Add garlic powder, salt, and pepper. Toss in bowl until coated.

Place in the air fryer basket and bake on 400 degrees for 8–12 minutes, turning florets once during baking. Check them at the 5-minute mark for desired tenderness. You don't want them to be wilted and overdone.

Remove florets from oven. Melt butter in medium glass bowl. Add hot sauce to butter. Toss cauliflower and stir to coat. Start with about half the sauce and add more to your taste.

Return to oven and cook for additional 5 minutes at 350 degrees.

Serve with any dip you like, ranch dressing, or blue cheese dip.

Tip: If you have a great gluten-free wing sauce, this recipe becomes gluten-free.

Buffalo Cauliflower, page 60

Garlic Parmesan Fries

1 tsp. olive oil

1 clove garlic, crushed

canola cooking spray

3 potatoes

4 tsp. fresh grated Parmesan cheese

salt and black pepper

Combine the oil and crushed garlic in a large bowl.

Cut the potato lengthwise into wedges (8 wedges for each potato). Rinse them in cold water and pat dry. Place them in a single layer on a microwavable plate and microwave for 1½ minutes on high.

Remove them from the microwave and place them in the bowl with garlic and oil. Toss in the grated cheese and coat evenly.

Season with salt and black pepper. Place in a single layer, in batches, in the air fryer basket. Bake at 400 degrees for about 10 minutes on each side, until golden brown.

Garlic Parmesan Fries, page 68

Air-Fried Avocados with Jalapeño Salsa, page 71

Air-Fried Avocados with Jalapeño Salsa

Salsa

3 tsp. olive oil

1 jalapeño chiles, diced and seeded

3 cups tomatoes, chopped

4 Tbsp. chopped cilantro

2 Tbsp. fresh lime juice

¼ tsp. salt and pepper

Avocados

2 eggs

½ cup flour

1½ cups panko bread crumbs

2 firm but ripe avocados, pitted, peeled, and each cut into 8 wedges

¼ tsp. each salt and pepper

For the Salsa

Combine oil, jalapeños, tomatoes, cilantro, lime juice, and salt and pepper in a medium bowl. Toss to mix well, and then set aside.

For the Avocados

To air fry the avocados, set up an assembly line to coat the avocados. Prepare 3 separate bowls. In a shallow bowl, beat the eggs. In the second bowl, mix the flour with the salt and pepper. Place panko in the third bowl.

Dip one slice of the avocado at a time in the egg. Let the excess drip off and dredge the avocado in the seasoned flour. Shake off any excess and finally coat the avocado in the panko, making sure to cover all sides. You may have to pat the crumbs onto the avocado. Set on a plate and repeat.

Spray lightly with oil from a mister or spray oil. Set inside the air fryer basket in a single layer without touching. Turn on air fryer at 400 degrees for 6-10 minutes, turning halfway through.

Top with a bit of the salsa (and if you are feeling a bit daring, some sour cream) and enjoy.

Mozzarella Cheese Sticks

12 mozzarella string cheese sticks

2 eggs, beaten

2 cups Italian seasoned
  breadcrumbs

½ cup grated Parmesan cheese

½ cup flour

canola oil

Open each package of string cheese. Separate the cheese sticks and freeze for 1 hour.

Put the eggs in a medium bowl. In a separate medium bowl, mix the breadcrumbs together with the Parmesan cheese.

Place the flour in a large ziplock bag.

Add the cheese sticks to the bag with the flour and shake to coat them.

Take each cheese stick out of the bag, dip it in the eggs, and then dip it in the breadcrumb mixture.

Put the cheese sticks in a single layer in the basket. Do not overcrowd.

Bake at 400 degrees for about 8 minutes, turning over halfway through.

Serve with your favorite marinara as a dipping sauce.

Mozzarella Cheese Sticks, page 72

Roasted Caprese Tomatoes with Basil Dressing, page 75

Roasted Caprese Tomatoes with Basil Dressing

4 large ripe tomatoes

1 Tbsp. olive oil

2 Tbsp. balsamic vinegar

1 tsp. sugar

salt and pepper

4 slices fresh mozzarella cheese, ½ inch thick

4 basil leaves

Dressing

20 large basil leaves

1 clove garlic

juice of ½ lemon

2 Tbsp. olive oil

salt to taste

Cut the tomatoes in half and place on a nonstick cookie sheet, cut-side up.

Drizzle the olive oil and balsamic vinegar over the tomatoes and sprinkle them with the sugar and salt and pepper.

Roast at 330 degrees for 10–18 minutes until the skins are blistered.

Remove from the oven and top each of the tomatoes with the mozzarella. Return to the oven and roast for another 5 minutes.

Remove the roasted tomatoes from the oven.

Place a large basil leaf on each of the bottom halves of the tomatoes. Top with the top half of the tomato.

To make the dressing, combine all the ingredients in a small food processor until the basil is finely chopped. Drizzle over the top of the tomatoes.

Parmesan Cream Corn

1 Tbsp. butter

2 tsp. flour

½ cup half-and-half

dash cayenne pepper

dash salt

10 ounces frozen corn

½ cup grated Parmesan cheese

Combine all ingredients in a bowl.

Place in a 6-inch square baking dish and bake for 15 minutes at 330 degrees.

Hush Hush Puppies

⅔ cup yellow cornmeal

⅓ cup flour

1 tsp. baking powder

¾ tsp. salt

⅛ tsp black pepper

½ cup finely chopped onion

⅓ cup milk

2 eggs, lightly beaten

2 Tbsp. butter, melted

Lightly grease a mini muffin pan or spray with nonstick cooking spray.

In a medium bowl, combine the cornmeal, flour, baking powder, salt, and pepper.

In a separate bowl, mix together the onion, milk, eggs, and butter. Fold the egg mixture into the flour mixture until the flour mixture is just moistened.

Spoon 1 tablespoon of the batter into each of the prepared mini muffin cups. Bake for 10 minutes at 330 degrees, or until the hush puppies are firm to the touch and golden brown around the edges. Bake in batches as needed.

Parmesan Cream Corn, page 76

Torn Bread Salad with Roasted Tomatoes and Goat Cheese

8 small shallots, quartered

1½ cups grape tomatoes

2½ Tbsp. extra-virgin olive oil, divided

salt and pepper

1 cup cubed pumpernickel bread (½-inch cubes)

1 Tbsp. mayonnaise

1 Tbsp. sherry vinegar

½ tsp. Dijon mustard

2 romaine hearts, cut crosswise into ½-inch ribbons

3 ounces goat cheese, crumbled

In a medium baking dish, toss the shallots with the tomatoes and 1 tablespoon olive oil and season with salt and pepper.

Place in an air fryer basket and bake at 370 degrees for 15 minutes, tossing halfway through. Pour into a large bowl and let cool.

Meanwhile, spread the pumpernickel cubes in the air fryer basket and toast for about 5 minutes at 330 degrees, until crisp. Let cool.

In a small bowl, whisk the remaining 1½ tablespoon olive oil with the mayonnaise, sherry vinegar, and mustard. Season with salt and pepper.

Toss the toasted pumpernickel croutons, shallots, tomatoes, and romaine with the dressing until coated.

Add the goat cheese, toss gently, and serve.

Jalapeños . . . Are Popping!

1 (8-oz.) pkg. cream cheese, softened

3 jalapeños, finely chopped

½ cup shredded cheddar cheese

coarse salt and pepper

24 refrigerated square wonton wrappers

vegetable oil spray

In a bowl, combine cream cheese, jalapeños, cheddar cheese, and salt and pepper to taste.

In a mini muffin pan, arrange the wontons in each muffin cup. Add 1 teaspoon of the filling to the center of each wonton.

Place on the fryer rack and lightly spray them with the vegetable oil.

Air fry at 350 degrees for 8–10 minutes until golden.

Parmesan Artichoke Hearts

1 (15-oz.) can artichoke hearts, packed in water

2 eggs

1 cup panko breadcrumbs

¼ cup grated Parmesan cheese

Drain the artichokes and quarter.

Mix the eggs in a medium bowl. In a separate bowl, add the panko bread-crumbs and Parmesan cheese and mix well.

Dip each artichoke in the eggs, and then coat them with the panko mixture.

Place on small plate and spray both sides lightly with canola oil.

Place in the air fryer basket in a single layer and bake at 400 degrees for 10 minutes, turning halfway through. Bake in batches as needed.

Tip: These can be made gluten-free by substituting crushed Rice Chex cereal for the panko.

Roasted Parmesan Cauliflower

2 cups cauliflower florets

½ medium onion, sliced thin

4 sprigs fresh thyme

4 cloves garlic, unpeeled

3 Tbsp. olive oil

salt and pepper, to taste

½ cup Parmesan cheese

Toss all the ingredients except the cheese in a large bowl.

Place in an air fryer basket and bake at 350 degrees for 25 minutes, tossing halfway through.

Once the cauliflower is cooked through, place it in a bowl and toss with the Parmesan cheese.

Greek Potatoes

½ tsp. salt

½ tsp. black pepper

½ tsp. paprika

½ tsp. dried oregano

3 garlic cloves, chopped

2 Tbsp. butter, melted

1 Tbsp. lime juice

1½ cups chicken broth

2 large baking potatoes, peeled, washed, and cut into wedges

1 cup grated Parmesan cheese

1 cup chopped parsley leaves

In a large bowl, mix the salt, pepper, paprika, oregano, garlic, butter, lime juice, and chicken broth together. After completely mixed, add the potatoes to the bowl.

Place the mixture in a baking dish. Then place the dish inside the air fryer basket. Cover with foil. Bake at 400 degrees for 20 minutes.

Uncover and sprinkle with the Parmesan cheese. Bake for another 8 minutes at 370 degrees. Sprinkle with the chopped parsley leaves.

Roasted Parmesan Cauliflower, page 82

Roasted Red Potato Salad with Mustard Vinaigrette (Cold or Hot), page 85

Roasted Red Potato Salad with Mustard Vinaigrette (Cold or Hot)

Roasted Red Potatoes

1½ lb. red potatoes, quartered

4 cloves garlic, diced

2 Tbsp. olive oil

salt and pepper

Vinaigrette

2 Tbsp. olive oil

1 Tbsp. grainy mustard

1 Tbsp. white wine vinegar

2 Tbsp. chopped parsley

salt and pepper

For the Potatoes

Add the potatoes and garlic to a bowl, drizzle with the oil, tossing to coat, and sprinkle with salt and pepper.

Place the potatoes in the air fryer basket. Roast the potatoes until crisp and golden brown on the outside and tender on the inside, about 15–20 minutes at 370 degrees, flipping halfway through.

For the Vinaigrette

While the potatoes are roasting, make the vinaigrette: Whisk together the oil, mustard, white wine vinegar, and parsley. Season with salt and pepper.

Toss the still-hot potatoes with the vinaigrette and serve warm. (Or keep in the refrigerator and serve them cold.)

Spicy Roasted Rosemary Nuts

1 cup almonds

1 cup pecans

1 cup cashew nuts

1 tsp. sea salt

2 Tbsp. finely chopped rosemary

½ tsp. cayenne pepper

2 tsp. brown sugar

2 Tbsp. butter, melted

In an air fryer basket, combine the almonds, pecans, and cashews. Bake at 330 degrees for about 18 minutes or until toasted, stirring once.

In a small bowl, combine the rosemary, brown sugar, salt, and cayenne pepper. Stir in butter.

Once the nuts are roasted, place them in a bowl with the rosemary mixture and gently toss to coat.

Serve them warm or cooled to room temperature. Store in an airtight container for up to 7 days.

Spicy Roasted Rosemary Nuts, page 86

Sweet Potato Fries—Any Which Way!, page 89

Sweet Potato Fries —Any Which Way!

2 lbs. sweet potatoes

¼ cup olive or other vegetable oil

1-2 Tbsp. sugar

1 Tbsp. salt

2 Tbsp. spice of choice

Peel the sweet potatoes and cut off the ends. Cut them in half lengthwise and then, if they are very long, in half crosswise. Cut each piece into wedges.

Rinse the potatoes with water. Place on a microwave-safe plate and microwave for 3 minutes on high.

Take the potatoes out and let them cool slightly.

Put the sweet potatoes into a large bowl and add the oil. Mix well to combine.

Sprinkle with the salt, sugar, and spices of your choice. Coat the potatoes well.

Spread the sweet potatoes out in a single layer. Bake at 400 degrees for 25 minutes, turning halfway through.

Note: Delicious and crispy—you add your own spice! Pick whatever you love! Here are a few suggestions: chipotle powder, smoked paprika, Chinese five-spice, pumpkin pie spice, garam masala, or Cajun seasoning.

Vegetable Chips

2 medium vegetables (beets,
zucchini, sweet potatoes,
squash, carrots, and so on)

1 tsp. extra-virgin olive oil

Peel your vegetables and slice them 1/16 inch thick with a mandoline. In a large bowl, toss sliced vegetables with extra-virgin olive oil. If you want to add a spice or salt and pepper, do so now.

In batches, lay the slices out in an air fryer basket. Bake at 400 degrees for 5 minutes. Open and toss. Bake for another 5 minutes until crisp. (You may need to cook slightly longer if you are using a vegetable with more water content.)

Stuffed Garlic Mushrooms

1 slice white bread

1 clove garlic, crushed

1 Tbsp. finely chopped flat leaf
parsley

salt and pepper

1 Tbsp. olive oil

12 mushrooms

In a food processor, grind the slice of bread into fine crumbs and mix in the garlic and parsley. Salt and pepper to taste. When fully mixed, stir in the olive oil.

Cut off the mushroom stems and fill the caps with the breadcrumbs. Pat the crumbs into the caps. Place the mushrooms in the air fryer basket and slide into the fryer.

Bake at 390 degrees for 10 minutes until golden and crispy.

Vegetable Chips, page 90

Zucchini Crunch Fries, page 93

Zucchini Crunch Fries

½ cup panko crumbs

¼ cup grated Parmesan cheese

¼ tsp. basil

¼ tsp. oregano

¼ tsp. cayenne pepper

2 medium-sized zucchini

¼ cup egg whites (about 2 egg whites)

In a bowl, mix together the crumbs, cheese, and herbs. Set aside.

Wash the zucchini well; leave unpeeled. Cut in half crosswise. Then cut into wedges not more than ½ inch thick.

Put the egg whites in a shallow bowl. Put a small amount of the crumb mixture on another plate.

Dip a zucchini wedge in the egg whites to coat. Then place it in the crumbs to coat, pressing down well. Place the wedges in a single layer in an air fryer pan.

Spray the wedges lightly with canola oil. Set temperature to 350 degrees and cook for 7 minutes. Turn wedges over with tongs, and cook for another 7 minutes.

Tip: These can be made gluten-free by substituting crushed Rice Chex cereal for the panko.

Soy Salmon Steaks

2 salmon fillets
black pepper and salt
⅛ tsp. garlic powder
lemon juice from 1 large lemon
⅓ cup light soy sauce

⅓ cup brown sugar
⅓ cup water
2 Tbsp. olive oil

Wash and pat the salmon dry with paper towels. Season the salmon fillets with black pepper, salt, and garlic powder.

In another bowl, stir together the lemon juice, soy sauce, brown sugar, water, and oil until sugar is dissolved.

Pour into a shallow dish. Place the salmon in the marinade. Cover and refrigerate for at least 2 hours.

Arrange the fish fillets on an air fryer grill basket. Bake at 330 degrees for 8 minutes or until done.

Tip: These can be made gluten-free by substituting a gluten-free soy sauce for the regular soy sauce.

Soy Salmon Steaks, page 102

Baked Lemon Chicken, page 105

Baked Lemon Chicken

¼ cup olive oil

3 Tbsp. minced garlic

⅓ cup white wine

1 Tbsp. grated lemon zest

2 Tbsp. freshly squeezed lemon juice

1½ tsp. dried oregano

1 tsp. minced fresh thyme leaves

kosher salt and freshly ground black pepper

4 boneless chicken breasts, skin on

1 lemon

Warm the olive oil in a small saucepan over medium-low heat. Add the garlic and cook for just 1 minute, but don't allow the garlic to turn brown.

Remove from the heat and add the white wine, lemon zest, lemon juice, oregano, thyme, and 1 teaspoon salt. Pour into a baking dish.

Pat the chicken breasts dry and place them skin side up in the sauce. Brush the chicken breasts with the olive oil and sprinkle them liberally with salt and pepper. Cut the lemon in 8 wedges and tuck it among the pieces of chicken.

Bake for 30 minutes at 330 degrees, depending on the size of the chicken breasts, until the chicken is done and the skin is lightly browned. Allow to rest for 5 minutes and serve.

Curried Lamb Chops

1 lb. loin lamb chops

2 Tbsp. olive oil

1 cup spinach

½ cup cilantro leaves

¼ cup plain Greek yogurt

¼ cup chicken stock

2 Tbsp. green curry paste

Season chops with salt and pepper. Place in air fryer basket at 400 degrees for 8-15 minutes until cooked to your choice of doneness. In blender, purée remaining ingredients. Spoon over lamb.

Curried Lamb Chops, page 106

Crispy Asian Dumplings, page 109

Crispy Asian Dumplings

24 round wonton wrappers

Filling

4 cups shredded cabbage

1 Tbsp. minced green onions

¼ cup chopped water chestnuts

1 lb. ground pork, cooked and crumbled

1 Tbsp. soy sauce

½ Tbsp. freshly grated ginger

1 tsp. sesame oil

In a large bowl, combine filling ingredients.

Place a wrapper on work surface and drop 1 heaping teaspoon of filling in the center.

Moisten edges with water using your fingertip and fold the dumpling in half and pinch to seal. Repeat with remaining dumplings.

Place the dumplings in an air fryer in batches. Spray them lightly with canola oil and bake at 400 degrees for 10 minutes, turning over halfway through.

Serve the dumplings hot with any of your favorite dipping sauces.

Garlic Ginger Shrimp, page 113

Garlic Ginger Shrimp

2 cloves garlic, chopped

1 tsp. grated ginger

2 green onions, chopped

2 tsp. fresh squeezed lime juice

2 Tbsp. soy sauce

1½ Tbsp. sugar

3 Tbsp. butter

1 lb. shrimp, cleaned

In a small saucepan, mix all ingredients except the shrimp. Heat to simmer. Then remove from heat and let cool. This can be done a day ahead.

Place the shrimp and marinade in a bag or bowl covered in plastic wrap and marinade for at least an hour in the fridge.

Place the shrimp on a single layer in the air fryer basket. Spritz with a light coat of canola oil.

Bake at 350 degrees for 8 minutes, turning halfway through. You may need to adjust the time, depending on the size of the shrimp.

Crunchy Taco Cups

1 lb. ground beef, browned and drained

1 envelope taco seasoning

1 (10-oz.) can diced tomatoes and chilies, drained

1 jalapeño, diced

24 wonton wrappers

1 cup shredded cheddar cheese

Combine the beef, seasoning mix, diced tomatoes, and jalapeño in a bowl and mix well.

In a mini muffin pan, line all the muffin cups with a wonton wrapper. Spritz with canola oil. Add 1 tablespoon of beef filling to each and top with the cheese.

Bake at 370 for 8-10 minutes until hot and golden.

Dill Salmon on Cedar Paper

1 tsp. olive oil

¼ tsp. lemon pepper seasoning

¼ tsp. dried dill

¼ tsp. fennel seeds, chopped

½ teaspoon salt

2 (6-oz.) salmon fillets

1 sheet cedar paper

In a small bowl, whisk together olive oil, lemon pepper, dill, fennel seeds, and salt. Add to a resealable plastic bag along with the salmon, shaking the bag to coat the salmon. Refrigerate for 1 hour.

Cut the cedar paper to fit inside of the air fryer basket. Place the salmon on the paper skin-side up. Bake at 350 degrees for 5–10 minutes, turning halfway through until done to your liking.

Dill Salmon on Cedar Paper, page 114

Grilled Cheese Perfection, page 117

Grilled Cheese Perfection

2 slices bread per sandwich

3 slices cheese, your choice

butter

Butter each slice of bread on both sides.

Place one slice of buttered bread on the rack. Add the cheese slices on top of the bread. Cover the cheese with the second slice of buttered bread.

Bake at 400 degrees for 8 minutes, turning halfway through.

Note: You choose the cheese—brie, cheddar, American, swiss, provolone . . . it doesn't matter! Also, it is great to use this as a base and start adding in your own favorite toppings like onion jam, arugula, and so on.

Buffalo Chicken Bowls

2 Tbsp. wing sauce (mild or hot, according to taste)

¼ cup softened cream cheese

2 Tbsp. ranch salad dressing or blue cheese dressing

6 ounces cooked chicken breasts, diced

1½ ounces blue cheese, crumbled

12 wonton wrappers

extra blue cheese, for topping

In a large bowl, mix together the hot wing sauce, softened cream cheese, and ranch dressing. Add in the chicken and blue cheese. Stir until just combined.

In a mini muffin pan, place 1 wonton wrapper in each mini muffin cup. Press down until it creates a cup.

Fill each wrapper cup ¾ of the way with the chicken mixture.

Bake for 10 minutes at 330 degrees, or until the wrappers are golden brown and the cheese is bubbling. Top with more crumbled blue cheese for garnish.

Garlic Rosemary Steak

2 steaks, 8 ounces each (can be
   any kind of steak)

3 sprigs rosemary, finely chopped

3 cloves garlic, finely chopped   olive oil

pinch red pepper flakes   salt and pepper

In a small bowl, combine the rosemary, garlic, red pepper flakes, and enough olive oil to make a loose paste.

Spread the mixture over both sides of each steak and sprinkle them generously with salt and pepper. Let them marinate for about 20 minutes.

Place the steaks in the air fryer basket. How long you should cook them depends on how you like your steak. Keep a close eye on these. I like to go with a thicker steak to have it more rare.

Roast at 400 degrees until your preferred doneness, about 15 minutes. Turn the steak halfway through your cooking time.

Garlic Rosemary Steak, page 118

Sweet-and-Sticky Sriracha Chicken

2 Tbsp. olive oil

1½ Tbsp. soy sauce

1½ Tbsp. balsamic vinegar

1 Tbsp. honey

2 cloves garlic, chopped

½ tsp. crushed red pepper

1 lemon, zested and juiced

6-8 chicken thighs and legs

sriracha for drizzling

In a large bowl, whisk together the olive oil, soy, balsamic, honey, garlic, red pepper, lemon zest, and juice.

Place the chicken in the bowl with the sauce and let marinate for 10-30 minutes, turning occasionally.

Place chicken in air fryer basket in a single layer and bake at 350 degrees for 12-24 minutes, depending on the size until cooked through, turning halfway through cooking. Top with a drizzle of sriracha.

Tip: These can be made gluten-free by substituting a gluten-free soy sauce for the regular soy sauce.

Sweet-and-Sticky Sriracha Chicken, page 120

Cod with Spring Vegetables in Parchment

½ cup cherry tomatoes

½ cup green beans, quartered

2 Tbsp. extra-virgin olive oil

1 small zucchini, sliced thin

1 carrot, julienned

½ red onion, sliced thin

1 clove garlic, finely chopped

1 tsp. herbs de provence

½ large lemon, cut into 4 slices

2 (6-oz.) fillets cod or sea bass

2 Tbsp. white wine

Place the tomatoes and green beans in the basket of the air fryer and spritz with olive oil with salt and pepper. Roast at 350 degrees until the tomatoes burst and the beans are tender, 5–7 minutes.

Cut 4 pieces of parchment paper that are double the size of the bottom of the air fryer. In a large bowl, combine the zucchini, carrots, onion, garlic, and herbs de provence. Divide the seasoned vegetables among the pieces of parchment. Top each with 2 lemon slices, tomatoes, and green beans, and a piece of fish. Put 1 tablespoon of wine and extra-virgin olive oil on each.

To seal, fold over the long sides of the parchment together twice, then roll in the short sides to form a pouch.

Roast until the fish is just opaque, about 12 minutes at 300 degrees.

Cheeseburger-Stuffed Baked Potatoes

Cheese Sauce

2 tsp. butter

2 tsp. flour

¼ tsp. salt

⅛ tsp. black pepper

½ cup milk

10 slices American cheese

Filling

½ lb. ground beef

¼ cup diced onion

⅛ tsp. salt

⅛ tsp. black pepper

1 tsp. Worcestershire sauce

4 Tbsp. ketchup

3 potatoes, baked and cooled

To prepare the cheese sauce, melt the butter in a small saucepan. Add the flour and cook, while stirring, for about 1 minute. Add the salt, pepper, and milk. Bring the mixture to a simmer, stirring constantly. When the sauce has thickened, remove from the heat and add the cheese. Stir until the cheese is completely melted.

To prepare the filling, brown the ground beef with the onion in a small sauté pan over medium heat. Drain off the extra fat and place the meat into a large bowl. Mix in the salt, black pepper, Worcestershire sauce, ketchup, and cheese sauce to the bowl and set aside.

Cut an opening in each baked potato lengthwise, starting from the top of each potato.

Scoop out the flesh, creating a shell. Take half of the potato flesh and chop it into small pieces and set aside. (Feel free to use the other half of the potato flesh from this recipe in the Crispy Cheesy Hash Brown Casserole on page 10.) Repeat with each potato. Place the empty potato shells into the air fryer basket.

Mix the reserved potato flesh with the beef mixture. Fill the potato shells with the mixture.

Bake at 330 degrees for 15–18 minutes.

Pepperoni Pizza Rolls

2 Tbsp. olive oil

½ cup diced zucchini

½ cup chopped red bell pepper

4 medium mushrooms, sliced

6 ounces pepperoni, sliced

6 ounces pizza sauce

12 egg roll wrappers

8 ounces mozzarella cheese, shredded

Heat the olive oil over medium heat in a medium-size skillet. Add the zucchini, pepper, and mushrooms to the skillet and sauté until soft.

Remove the pan from the heat and let the vegetables cool slightly. Then spoon the vegetables and 10 slices of pepperoni into a food processor with the pizza sauce.

Pulse until the vegetables are roughly chopped.

Lay out each of the egg roll wrappers. Lay 4 sliced pepperoni on each wrapper on the top ⅓ of the wrapper, leaving ¼ inch on each side of wrapper.

Place 1 tablespoon of the filling on top of the pepperoni and top with 1 tablespoon cheese. Fold the 2 sides in and then roll up in thirds. It is the same as rolling an egg roll.

Place the roll in the air fryer basket and spritz with canola oil.

Bake at 370 degrees for 8 minutes.

Perfect Pork Chop with Spinach and Kale Salad, page 137

Perfect Pork Chop with Spinach and Kale Salad

½ cup apple cider vinegar

1 Tbsp. whole grain mustard

2 Tbsp. honey

½ cup olive oil

pepper

salt

2½ cups thinly sliced kale leaves, center ribs removed

1 cup baby spinach

1 Granny Smith apple, cut into matchsticks

4 center-cut loin pork chops, each about 2 inches thick

4 tsp. fresh thyme

2 tsp. dried marjoram

For the Dressing and Salad

Mix together the vinegar, mustard, and honey in a small bowl. Gradually add in the olive oil and add a pinch of salt and pepper.

In a separate bowl, combine the kale, spinach, and apple. Add the dressing and toss to coat. Let stand for at least 5–8 minutes before serving.

For the Pork Chops

Season the meat on both sides with salt and pepper, thyme, and marjoram.

Place the pork chops in the air fryer basket. Bake at 400 degrees for 20 minutes, turning halfway through. Use an instant read thermometer to measure 145 degrees for doneness.

Mound the salad on a platter and top with the pork chops.

Steam-Roasted Herb Mussels

1 lb. mussels

½ cup white wine

2 Tbsp. butter, softened

1 small clove garlic, minced

¼ cup fresh flat-leaf parsley, very finely chopped

⅛ tsp. smoked paprika

Clean the mussels by placing them in a large bowl of cold water and soaking for 8-10 minutes. Remove each clam individually and scrub under running water. Discard any clams with chipped shells or that are not completely shut.

In a baking dish that fits into the air fryer, put the butter, white wine, garlic, and paprika. Bake at 350 for 2-3 minutes until bubbly and hot.

Put the mussels into the air fryer inside of the baking dish with butter mixture and toss. Bake at 350 for 3-10 minutes, checking to see if the clams are opening.

Check every 3 minutes, removing open shells until all clams have opened, setting them aside. Let them cool slightly.

When all the clams are open, return the wine butter sauce and toss. Serve warm.

Steam-Roasted Shell Herb Mussels, page 138

Lemon shrimp with Spicy Tarragon Dipping Sauce, page 141

Lemon Shrimp with Spicy Tarragon Dipping Sauce

Spicy Dip

1 cup mayonnaise

1 Tbsp. shallots, minced

zest of 1 orange

1 Tbsp. fresh orange juice

1 Tbsp. fresh lemon juice

2 Tbsp. fresh tarragon, chopped

¼ tsp. salt

¼ tsp. black pepper

½ tsp. hot pepper sauce

Shrimp

1 lb. shrimp

½ tsp. ground coriander

⅛ tsp. ground white pepper

½ cup white wine

½ cup water

½ tsp. minced garlic

¼ tsp. mustard seed

3 orange slices

juice of half a lemon

For the Dipping Sauce

Combine the mayonnaise, shallots, orange zest, orange and lemon juice, tarragon, salt, pepper, and hot pepper sauce in a bowl. Cover it and refrigerate the mixture for at least 1 hour.

For the Lemon Shrimp

Toss the shrimp with the coriander and pepper in a bowl.

In the bottom of your "bowl," under the air fryer basket, pour in white wine. Place the garlic, mustard seed, and lemon juice. Place air fryer basket insert back into place. Turn oven on without shrimp for 5 minutes at 350 degrees.

Put 3 large orange slices into the basket and top with the shrimp.

Bake at 350 degrees for 6-10 minutes to air steam the shrimp, turning halfway through cooking.

You can serve them warm or refrigerate until chilled. Serve with the dipping sauce.

Roasted Italian Sausage, Peppers, and Onions, page 145

Roasted Italian Sausage, Peppers, and Onions

1 lb. red potatoes, cut into large chunks

1 onion, cut into wedges

1 yellow pepper, cut into wedges

1 red bell pepper, cut lengthwise

3 sprigs rosemary

1 Tbsp. olive oil

1 lb. Italian sausage

Place all the cut vegetables and rosemary in a large bowl. Drizzle with oil and coat thoroughly.

Arrange the potatoes, onion wedges, peppers, and rosemary on the bottom of the air fryer basket. Then place the sausage on top of the vegetables.

Roast for 30–35 minutes at 370 degrees or until potatoes are fork tender and sausages are lightly browned, stirring once halfway through.

Note: The trick here is to cut everything about the same size so they cook evenly.

Famous Meatballs

1 lb. lean ground beef

4 ounces ground pork

1 cup Italian-flavored breadcrumbs

½ cup milk

¼ cup fresh parsley leaves, finely chopped

2 eggs, lightly beaten

1 clove garlic, minced

½ medium onion, minced

½ cup Parmesan cheese, grated

salt and pepper to taste

In a large bowl or mixer, thoroughly mix all ingredients until evenly mixed. Chill in the refrigerator for 30 minutes to 1 hour.

Shape into meatballs and place on air fryer basket in a single layer. Bake 12–18 minutes at 350 degrees.

Fantastic on their own, but add a little sauce and these will sing on a sub or with pasta!

Famous Meatballs, page 146

White Pizzas with Chicken, page 149

White Pizzas with Chicken

15 ounces refrigerated, fresh pizza dough, divided

Oil

¼ cup olive oil

2 Tbsp. chopped fresh basil

½ tsp. crushed red pepper

4 garlic cloves, crushed

4 fresh thyme sprigs

Topping

1 cup ricotta cheese

Pizzas

6 ounces shredded, cooked chicken breasts

2 ounces shredded Italian-blend cheese

3 ounces fresh mozzarella cheese, torn into small pieces

1 Tbsp. fresh thyme leaves

1 tsp. freshly ground black pepper

¼ cup small fresh basil, for garnish

Combine oil, basil, red pepper, garlic cloves, and thyme sprigs in a small saucepan over medium heat. Cook 4 minutes or until garlic begins to brown, stirring frequently. Remove from heat; let stand 5 minutes. Strain mixture through a fine sieve over a small bowl; discard solids.

Divide dough into equal pieces that when rolled out will fit in the bottom of your air fryer basket. Roll each piece into a circle on a lightly floured surface. Spritz one side of the dough with olive oil and place oil side down inside the air fryer basket. Spread about 1 tablespoons oil mixture over each pizza, leaving a ½-inch border. Divide chicken, Italian-blend cheese, and mozzarella cheese evenly among pizzas; sprinkle evenly with thyme leaves and black pepper.

Bake at 450 degrees for 6–10 minutes or until dough is golden and cheese browns. Repeat procedure with remaining pizzas. Sprinkle pizzas evenly with fresh basil leaves.

Philly Steak Rolls

1 green bell pepper, finely chopped

1 medium white onion, finely chopped

1 (6-oz.) pkg. frozen Philly-style sliced steak

½ lb. shredded provolone cheese

12 egg roll wrappers

Sauté the pepper and onion in a large pan, with a drizzle of olive oil, until they are slightly softened but still crisp, about 5–6 minutes. Set aside on a paper towel–lined plate until cooled.

In the same pan, heat the sliced meat until cooked through. Use a spatula to chop up the meat as it cooks. Cook until browned and transfer to a paper towel-lined plate until cooled.

When the meat and vegetables are cooled, add them into a large bowl with the shredded cheese. Stir to combine.

On a clean, dry surface like a cutting board, lay out your egg roll wrappers. You should only lay a few out at a time so that they do not dry out. Place ¼ cup of the meat mixture in the center of each wrapper.

Fold ⅓ of the wrapper over, fold both sides in toward the middle, and then fold over on itself. It will resemble an egg roll.

Spritz the outside with canola or olive oil spray.

Set your temperature to 350 degrees and bake for 10 minutes. Then set it to 400 degrees for another 2 minutes.

Rosemary Pork Chops & Potatoes

4 Tbsp. vegetable oil, divided

2 Tbsp. chopped fresh rosemary

1 tsp. dried oregano

1 tsp. dried basil

1½ tsp. salt, divided

¾ tsp. ground black pepper, divided

zest of ½ orange

12 small red bliss potatoes, washed and quartered into wedges

1 Tbsp. chopped garlic

4 boneless pork chops, cut 1 inch thick

To prepare the rub for the pork, combine 1 tablespoon oil, rosemary, oregano, basil, 1 teaspoon salt, ½ teaspoon black pepper, and orange zest in a small bowl; mix well. Set aside.

To prepare the potatoes, combine the potatoes, 1 tablespoon oil, garlic, ½ teaspoon salt, ¼ teaspoon black pepper, and 1 teaspoon of the rosemary rub in a large bowl. Toss potatoes until well coated; set aside.

To prepare the pork chops, evenly coat each chop with the remaining rosemary rub.

Place the potatoes in the bottom of the air fryer basket. Place the chops on top of the potatoes in a single layer.

Bake at 350 degrees for 30 minutes or until done, turning halfway through.

Shrimp & Cream Cheese Wontons

8 ounces shrimp, peeled, deveined, and roughly chopped

4 ounces cream cheese, room temperature

2 cloves garlic, minced

2 green onions, thinly sliced

1 Tbsp. freshly grated ginger

1 tsp. sesame oil

1 tsp. sriracha (optional)

salt and pepper

16 (2-inch) wonton wrappers

1 large egg, beaten

In a large bowl, combine the shrimp, cream cheese, garlic, green onions, ginger, sesame oil, and sriracha, if using. Season with salt and pepper to taste.

To assemble the wontons, place the wrappers on a work surface. Spoon 1½ teaspoons of the mixture into the center of each wrapper. Using your finger, rub the edges of the wrappers with the beaten egg.

Fold all sides over the filling to create an "X," pinching the edges to seal.

Place the prepared wontons in a single layer in an air fryer basket. Coat the wontons with nonstick spray.

Bake for 10–12 minutes at 370 degrees, or until golden brown and crisp.

Shrimp & Cream Cheese Wonton Dipping Sauce

3 Tbsp. honey

2 Tbsp. low-sodium soy sauce

1 Tbsp. sriracha or other hot sauce

1 tsp. vinegar or rice wine vinegar

¼ tsp. sesame oil

Mix together and serve.

Shrimp & Cream Cheese Wontons, page 152

Shrimp with Roasted Garlic-Cilantro Sauce, page 155

Shrimp with Roasted Garlic-Cilantro Sauce

1½ lb. shrimp, raw and cleaned

Sauce

1 small head garlic

olive oil, for drizzling

1 cup chopped fresh cilantro leaves

juice of 1 lime

1 Tbsp. white wine

3 Tbsp. olive oil

2 Tbsp. chili sauce (or 1 Tbsp. dry chili flakes)

Trim the top of the garlic head off, but leave the garlic intact. Place on a 12 × 12-inch piece of foil. Drizzle generously with olive oil. Wrap up garlic inside of foil to seal all the edges.

Place the foil in the air fryer basket and roast the garlic at 400 degrees for about 10-15 minutes or until slightly tender and fragrant. When ready, remove from the air fryer. Let cool.

When the garlic is cool enough to handle, squeeze the roasted garlic out of its peel and chop finely.

In a small bowl, combine the roasted garlic with the remaining sauce ingredients. Whisk together and set aside.

In a separate bowl, place shrimp and 2 tablespoons of the sauce mix. Toss to coat shrimp.

Place the shrimp in a single layer on the bottom of the air fryer basket. Bake at 370 degrees for 6-10 minutes, turning halfway. Bake in batches as needed.

Remove the shrimp from the basket and add to a bowl, coating well with the remaining roasted garlic-cilantro sauce.

Southern Buttermilk-Fried Chicken

2 chicken breasts (or legs or thighs, your preference)

Marinade

2 cups buttermilk

2 tsp. salt

2 tsp. black pepper

1 tsp. cayenne pepper

Seasoned Flour

2 cups flour

1 Tbsp. baking powder

1 Tbsp. garlic powder

1 Tbsp. paprika powder

1 tsp. salt

1 tsp. pepper

Rinse the chicken and pat dry with paper towels.

For the Marinade

Toss together the chicken pieces, black pepper, cayenne pepper, and salt in a large bowl to coat. Pour the buttermilk over the chicken until it is coated. Refrigerate for at least 6 hours or overnight.

For the Seasoned Flour

In separate bowl, combine the flour, baking powder, garlic powder, paprika, salt, and pepper. Remove the chicken 1 piece at a time from the buttermilk, and dredge in the seasoned flour. Shake off any excess flour and transfer to a plate.

Arrange the chicken in 1 layer in the fryer basket with the skin-side up, spray with canola oil, and slide the basket into the air fryer.

Bake at 370 degrees for 20 minutes. Pull out the tray, turn the chicken pieces over, spray the other side, and bake for another 10 minutes.

Tip: These can be made gluten-free by substituting a gluten-free flour (recipe found on page xvi) for the regular flour.

Southern Buttermilk-Fried Chicken, page 156

Sweet and Sour Glazed Halibut, page 167

Sweet-and-Sour Glazed Halibut

½ cup fresh cilantro, minced, divided

1-inch piece ginger, peeled, minced

1½ Tbsp. soy sauce

1 Tbsp. fresh lime juice plus lime wedges for serving

½ tsp. honey

2 (8-oz.) halibut steaks at 1 inch thick, skinless

salt and pepper

1 Tbsp. toasted sesame oil

In a small bowl, combine ¼ cup cilantro, ginger, soy sauce, lime juice, and honey.

Season the halibut with salt and pepper. Place the halibut in the cilantro mixture and completely coat. Place the fish in a single layer in the air fryer basket. Pour the remaining cilantro mixture on top and roast until the fish is opaque in the center, 10–15 minutes at 350 degrees. Drizzle the sesame oil over the fish; sprinkle the remaining ¼ cup cilantro on top. Serve with the lime wedges.

Tip: Make this recipe gluten-free by substituting a gluten-free soy sauce for the regular soy sauce.

Bang Bang Shrimp

Coating

½ cup whole milk

1 egg, beaten lightly

2 Tbsp. cornstarch

1 tsp. salt

½ tsp. garlic powder

½ tsp. cayenne pepper

½ tsp. sugar

½ tsp. paprika

½ tsp. sriracha

Breading

1 cup panko breadcrumbs

1 lb. shrimp, peeled and deveined

Dipping Sauce

2 Tbsp. sriracha

2 Tbsp. ketchup

¼ cup mayonnaise

Mix all the coating ingredients together in a shallow baking dish.

In a separate dish, place the panko breadcrumbs.

Dip each shrimp in the coating batter and then in the breadcrumbs. Do this one at a time and place them into the air fryer basket in a single layer. Spritz with oil.

Bake at 400 degrees for 10 minutes, turning halfway through.

Repeat with remaining shrimp.

While the shrimp are cooking, mix all dipping sauce ingredients together.

Desserts

Three-Ingredient Brownies, page 173

Three-Ingredient Brownies

¾ cup Nutella   ¼ cup flour

1 egg

Mix all ingredients together. Using a nonstick spray, lightly spray a 6-inch metal round or square pan to fit in your air fryer.

Spread mixture around the pan with a spatula and bake for 10–12 minutes at 330 degrees.

Crispy Nutella Ravioli

16 wonton wrappers   1 cup Nutella

1 egg, lightly beaten   ½ cup sugar

Place 1 wonton wrapper on a work surface. Brush the edges of the wrapper lightly with the beaten egg. Spoon 1 tablespoon of Nutella into the center of the wrapper. Fold the wrapper diagonally in half over the filling and press the edges of the wrapper to seal.

Repeat with the remaining wonton wrappers, egg, and Nutella.

Place the sugar on a plate.

Spray each side of the prepared wontons with a nonstick vegetable oil spray and dip each side into the sugar.

Working in batches, place a single layer in the air fryer basket and spray with nonstick spray.

Bake at 370 degrees for 8 minutes, turning over halfway through.

Cherry Hand Pies

½ cup powdered sugar
¼ tsp. ground cinnamon
pinch of nutmeg

1 can large flaky-style biscuit dough
1 (12-oz.) can cherry pie filling

In a shallow dish, mix the sugar, ground cinnamon, and nutmeg.

Roll out each section of the biscuit dough into an 8-inch round circle with a rolling pin or bottle.

Put a large spoonful of pie filling into the center of the dough. Fold over 1 side and pinch tight.

Roll the filled dough in the sugar mixture. Spray each side lightly with canola oil and place in the air fryer basket so they are not touching.

In batches, bake at 330 degrees for 10–13 minutes until golden.

Cherry Hand Pies, page 174

All Season Fruit Cobbler, page 177

All Season Fruit Cobbler

½ cup flour

¼ cup sugar

¼ cup brown sugar

4 Tbsp. butter, cold and cut into cubes

1 lb. plums, peaches, or nectarines (or a combination), pitted and cut lengthwise into ½-inch wedges

Pulse all ingredients except the fruit in a food processor until mixture begins to clump.

Spread the fruit in a baking dish and sprinkle the topping over it. You can do one large baking dish or individual ones.

Bake at 330 degrees for 17–22 minutes until golden. It will depend on the size of the fruit used.

Spanish Fried Bananas

½ cup flour

¼ tsp. salt

2 eggs, whisked

¾ cup breadcrumbs

cinnamon sugar, optional

2 large bananas

Place the flour and salt in one bowl, the eggs in another, and the breadcrumbs in a third. The cinnamon sugar should go in another bowl if you choose to use it.

Peel the bananas and cut each one into thirds. Roll the bananas in the flour, then in the egg, and finally in the breadcrumbs. Drizzle a little olive oil in a shallow dish and quickly roll the bananas in it.

Place 4–5 pieces directly into the air fryer basket and bake at 350 degrees for 8 minutes. At 4 minutes, take the basket out and give it a little shake to move the bananas. Continue frying, and then remove the finished bananas and drop them directly into the cinnamon sugar or onto a serving plate. Allow to cool for 1 minute.

Note: Make your own cinnamon sugar by combining ½ cup sugar and ¼ teaspoon cinnamon.

Grilled Peach Splits

Cream Topping

½ cup whipping cream

1 Tbsp. powdered sugar

2 Tbsp. crème fraîche

¼ tsp. vanilla extract

Peaches

4 large firm-ripe peaches, halved and pitted

2-3 Tbsp. maple syrup

1 tsp. sugar

½ tsp. of chopped thyme leaves

1 tsp. of cinnamon

Baste the peach halves with the maple syrup and sprinkle with the sugar, thyme, and cinnamon combination. Place inside the air fryer basket cut-side up. Bake at 350 for 8-10, turning them halfway through until lightly browned.

For the cream topping, mix all ingredients together with a whisk or spoon until smooth.

Serve topped with cream topping over the warm peaches.

Tip: Try this technique will all types of fruit, like pineapple, plums, oranges, and mangos!

Grilled Peach Splits, page 178

Chocolate Molten Lava Cakes, page 181

Chocolate Molten Lava Cakes

⅓ cup butter, plus more for greasing the ramekins

cocoa powder, for dusting

½ cup chocolate chips or chopped chocolate

¼ cup sugar

2 Tbsp. flour

2 eggs

Grease the inside of 4 (8-oz.) ramekins with the butter, dust with the cocoa powder, and tap out any extra.

Place the chocolate chips and butter in a medium microwave-safe bowl and microwave in 30-second increments, stirring between each increment until the chocolate is melted and smooth.

Stir the sugar and flour into the chocolate mixture. Add in the eggs and mix until smooth.

Pour the batter into the 4 ramekins; they should be about half full. Place the ramekins in an air fryer basket.

Bake at 330 degrees for 12–15 minutes, until the top and edges are set but the center is still jiggly. Let cool slightly for 2–3 minutes. Be careful, because ramekins may still be hot. Serve immediately.

Jam Baked Apples

2 apples (I recommend Fuji or McIntosh)

1 tsp. lemon juice

¼ cup strawberry jam, jelly, or preserves

2 Tbsp. flour

3 Tbsp. butter, cold and diced

3 Tbsp. brown sugar

½ cup uncooked oats

¼ tsp. ground cinnamon

pinch of salt

Cut each apple in half along its equator. Using a melon baller, cut out each side of the core, creating a rounded hole. Rub the inside of the open apple with lemon juice. Place 1 tablespoon of jam into each hole.

To make the topping, mix together the flour, butter, brown sugar, oats, cinnamon, and salt in a small bowl. Press this mixture on the top of each apple half, covering the jam.

Place the prepared apples in a baking dish filled with about ¼ inch water. Bake at 330 degrees until the tops are golden brown and the apples are tender, 20–30 minutes.

Jam Baked Apples, page 182

Nutella Flake Pastry, page 185

Nutella Flake Pastry

1 can refrigerated crescent dinner
  rolls

8 Tbsp. Nutella

1 egg, lightly beaten

Open the crescent roll can. Keep the large squares intact. You should have 4 per can. Pinch all the seams together.

Place 2 tablespoons of the Nutella in the center of each square and fold the dough over to make a triangle. Brush lightly with the beaten egg.

Bake in batches at 350 degrees for 10-12 minutes until golden.

Raspberry Brown Sugar Gratin

1 cup fresh raspberries (or your choice of berry)

1 cup crème fraîche (or you can use Greek yogurt)

¼ tsp. fresh lemon zest

½ cup dark brown sugar

Gently fold raspberries, zest, and crème fraîche together in a shallow baking dish. Press the brown sugar through a mesh colander so that it sprinkles evenly over the dish.

Place your baking dish in the air fryer basket at 400 degrees and bake until the sugar has just started caramelizing. You need to watch this carefully so that it does not burn.

When the caramelization happens, take it out and enjoy by itself or over ice cream.

Raspberry Brown Sugar Gratin, page 186

Lemon Sponge Cake, page 189

Lemon Sponge Cake

Cake

1 cup flour

1 cup sugar

8 ounces butter, room temperature

3 eggs

1 tsp. baking powder

1 Tbsp. lemon zest

Glaze

¼ cup powdered sugar, plus more for topping

2 Tbsp. milk

2 Tbsp. lemon juice

Spray 2 (6-inch) metal baking pans with nonstick spray.

Place all the cake ingredients in a bowl and mix with a hand mixer until thick and creamy.

Place half of the batter in each pan. Bake at 350 degrees for 15 minutes until golden.

While baking, prepare glaze by mixing all the ingredients together. When the cakes are done, remove them from the air fryer and drizzle each cake with half of the glaze. Sprinkle with powdered sugar.

Chocolate Chip Mini Cheesecakes, page 197

Chocolate Chip Mini Cheesecakes

Crust

1 cup graham cracker crumbs

2 Tbsp. brown sugar

¼ tsp. salt

2½ Tbsp. butter, melted

Cheesecake

1 (8-oz.) pkg. cream cheese, softened

2 Tbsp. sour cream

⅓ cup sugar

1 egg

1 tsp. vanilla extract

1 cup chocolate chips

Line 8 cups of a mini muffin pan with paper liners.

For the Crust:

In a medium bowl, mix together the graham cracker crumbs, brown sugar, and salt. Pour melted butter over the mix and stir with a fork to moisten the crumb mixture.

Place about a tablespoon of the crumb mixture in each of the prepared muffin cups and pack down into an even layer.

For the Cheesecake:

In a large bowl, cream together the cream cheese, sour cream, and sugar until smooth. Beat in the egg and vanilla extract.

Place 1 tablespoon chocolate chips into each of the muffin cups. Evenly divide cheesecake batter between the muffin cups, covering the first layer of chocolate chips. Place another tablespoon of chocolate chips on top of the cheesecake batter in each of the muffin cups.

Bake for 18–23 minutes at 330 degrees, until cheesecakes are set. Bake in batches as needed.

Allow the cheesecakes to cool for 10 minutes in the muffin pan. Then carefully transfer the cheesecakes to a cooling rack to cool completely and store in the refrigerator.

Wild Berry Cheesecake Roll

1 (8-oz.) pkg. cream cheese

½ cup powdered sugar

1 tsp. vanilla extract

16 egg roll wrappers

2 cups chopped strawberries

2 cups blueberries

cinnamon sugar, for topping

Spray a baking sheet with nonstick cooking spray and set aside.

Combine the cream cheese, powdered sugar, and vanilla in a bowl and whip together.

Scoop about 1 tablespoon of the mixture onto an egg roll wrap that's been laid out on a clean dry surface. Next, add a small scoop of strawberries and blueberries.

Working the egg roll wrapper in a diamond configuration, roll the bottom corner up over the ingredients tightly. Next, fold the left and right sides over. Then finish rolling the wrapper. Use a little bit of water to seal the flap down.

Place a cheesecake roll on a baking sheet sprayed with nonstick spray. Spray each roll with nonstick spray and sprinkle with cinnamon sugar.

Bake in batches at 375 degrees for about 10 minutes or until golden brown. Turn over halfway through.

Wild Berry Cheesecake Roll, page 198

Apple Pie Roll-Ups

16 egg roll wrappers

1 (12-oz.) can apple pie filling

½ cup powdered sugar

1 Tbsp. cinnamon

⅛ tsp. nutmeg

4 Tbsp. butter, melted

Place the wraps on a clean, dry surface. Have each wrap facing out on the diagonal so that it is a diamond shape.

Place 2 tablespoons of the pie filling in the center of a wrapper. With your finger, seal the outside of all edges with water and fold up the wrapper like a burrito. Repeat with remaining wrappers.

Lightly spray with canola oil and place in a single layer, not touching, in the air fryer basket. Bake in batches at 350 degrees for 8–10 minutes until golden.

While baking, combine the powdered sugar, cinnamon, and nutmeg.

Remove the roll-ups from the basket and brush with melted butter. Sift the powdered sugar mixture on top while warm.

Easy Cannoli Cups

Wonton Cups

24 wonton wrappers

Filling

3 cups ricotta cheese

1⅓ cups powdered sugar

1 tsp. vanilla extract

⅓ cup semi-sweet mini chocolate chips

For the Wonton Cups

Place each wonton wrapper in the base of a mini cupcake pan, pressing down to create a mini bowl.

Bake at 350 degrees for 5 minutes until the cups are lightly browned.

Allow to cool fully before filling with the ricotta mixture.

For the Filling

Place the ricotta and vanilla in a medium-sized mixing bowl. Mix until smooth, about 2 minutes. Slowly add in the powdered sugar, mixing until just combined.

Stir in the chocolate chips. Fill the wonton cups ¾ full with filling and top with extra chips!

Index

About the Author

Allison Waggoner, top-rated television host, seen in more than 80 million homes, has recorded more than 80,000 hours of LIVE television, which is more than Oprah and Jay Leno combined! You can see Allison in the kitchen with celebrities such as Todd English, Paula Deen, and Sig Hanson. You've seen her on The Food Network's *Unwrapped*, and you can currently join in with her on *Evine Live*. Just in case you didn't know her true passion, it's FOOD and sharing it with YOU! As a classically trained chef, Allison's culinary and marketing career brought her to the attention of television executives. She first appeared as a guest host, bringing her confections and family culinary history to the home shopping world.

Growing up in the chocolate industry inspired a journey filled with delicious and innovative cuisine. Allison started with her family's gourmet chocolates, creating some of the finest award-winning confections in the world. Her culinary designs have been featured in Crate & Barrel, *Culinary Product Magazine*, Ghirardelli Chocolate Company, Godiva Chocolatier, Walt Disney World, *Fancy Food Magazine*, Target, Universal Studios, Williams-Sonoma, and on The Food Network.

Allison continues to bring her love of food and favorite recipes to you in this new edition of her bestselling *Air Fryer Cookbook*. Her book series, In the Kitchen, started with *A Collection of Home and Family Memories* and was released in 2014. Her second book, *A Gathering of Friends*, is a nostalgic collection of recipes to celebrate the moments in our lives and is filled with simple, delicious dishes for every day of the week.

Allison lives in the Twin Cities, Minnesota.

Visit her at www.allisonwaggoner.com